ZEN AND THE BASICS OF FINANCIAL ACCOUNTING

Financial Accounting by Simple Example

(Literally, a walk in the park)

Chux Kamalu

First published in 2014 by

Orisa Press

London N9 7JP

England.

Tel. +442088047677

©2014 E. C. Kamalu

Printed by Lulu: www.lulu.com

ISBN: 978-0-9557131-2-5

For Chiaka

CONTENTS

Acknowledgements

Thanks to Chiaka for proof reading, advice and moral support; to Kenneth for professional guidance; and to David and Shaun of the Book-keepers Forum for invaluable feedback.

1

INTRODUCTION

A while ago I realised, as I reached a certain stage in my career as a Finance Assistant that I could go no further without learning from a mentor to get just that step further ahead. My friend, Zen Zanto, had promised to show me how to do financial accounts. He had worked out a way in which he would be able to make me (even me) "get" financial accounts immediately, in his characteristic, Zen way of explanation.

I was quite anxious to get started. When I asked Zen when we should meet for this training, he said he would give me a call to arrange and that it was no big deal anyway, I should not worry. "It'll be a walk in the park!" he joked.

Next day when he called, it turned out he wasn't actually joking. We met in the park with our electronic tablets; me having downloaded a couple of financial accounts examples he had emailed to me.

"Let's chat financial accounts over a walk through the park" he said. "Let's use the journey through the park as a metaphor for the journey of learning financial accounts. And life itself!"

He doesn't half talk some nonsense sometimes, I thought to myself privately. I wanted a trainer, not a guru. But I decided I needed to give him all the space and flexibility he need to impart the knowledge I was hungry for, in his own typical manner – no matter how annoying. For a start: being trained on financial accounts on a tablet, walking through the park. Nice fresh air, scene and surroundings –

but bonkers, not practical. "How do I even take notes?" I said out loud.

Zen noted the irritation in my voice. "Exactly, I noticed you're great at note-taking but bad at listening. So this format, just for today, will help".

Zen was right, and I could not argue with Zen. Besides, I needed him to get on with it.

"In the guidance I am giving you, some basic knowledge of accounting principles is assumed. But the instruction does what it says on the tin: a guide that will ultimately teach the learner to prepare financial accounts as a stepping stone to the preparation of management accounts, by working through the simplest of examples. The examples are mostly applicable to charity accounting, but the principles are applicable universally. In essence, the learner is taught to prepare financial accounts by example: Two examples, to be precise. The teacher and student together go through the process of establishing a fictitious company in the books... Oops, that did not come out the way I intended that to sound ..." he added, on noticing my raised eyebrows at the suggestion of creating fictitious companies.

"... and performing the very first monthly financial accounts for this imaginary company, the Pyramid Company. By working through this concrete (although fictitious) example with the teacher, the student is taught, step by step, how to prepare a set of financial accounts".

"But then there is the Zen of Financial accounting. What can possibly be 'Zen' about financial accounting?"

I became confused: "Are you talking about yourself?" I enquired.

But he ignored me and continued: "By definition, Zen applies to daily life. So the Zen of financial accounting is merely to appreciate

the essential nature of financial accounting. The movement of assets and liabilities, income and expenditures reflect, in fact, the transactions and therefore movement of people.   Financial accounting is not simply about numbers, although numbers present their own wonder and fascination. Financial accounting is there to ensure resources are effectively managed and meet needs. In a Zen-like examination of financial accounting, it is a science which involves many processes from mundane data entry to the satisfaction of drafting a balance sheet, and all tasks will be performed with the same effort and presence of mind at all times, as far as possible."

"Oh, so you are talking about the philosophy of Zen?"

Still, he ignored me to continue his train. "It is plain, that the Zen philosophy or way of looking at life can be a great asset to making the job of the financial accountant more of a thing of daily wonder, because every task is used as an opportunity for meditation. This is meditation in the sense that the task is performed with such intense focus and concentration at the exclusion of outside distraction, that it is indeed a kind of meditation, but meditation in motion, which is in truth when meditation is a continuous state of not only mental discipline, but of calm and of lucidity of mind. If one can attain this state through their professional work, they have attained a form of "Nirvana" on this world, in this life, as we spend a good part of our lives in the work environment."

"In other words", said Zen Zanto, "the message of Zen and the Basics of Financial Accountancy is how this profession, like every profession offers the practitioner the scope for growth, not only in the acquisition of skills but also spiritual growth through doing even the littlest and most mundane tasks with diligence and presence of mind".

I thought to myself: I knew learning financial accounts would change my job prospects, but what was becoming apparent was that it would in fact change my life. Although initially sceptical, I was beginning to appreciate what Zen had to say and the way he chose to say it.

2

Beginnings: To Be or Not to Be...a Financial Accountant

In the early years of my secondary schooling in Cedarmouth, Avonshire, I was living in fear of the mathematics teacher, Mr Eudoxus, who was very severe looking and whose favourite tenet was "a thing of beauty is a joy forever".

As my classmates and I noted, with mischievous amusement, his other great saying, which we never tired of mimicking, bellowed in Mr Eudoxus's deep northern English accent was: "close those windows!" This was on account of the fact that Eudoxus hated the cold and felt it intensely. So his first acts on entering a cold draughty classroom were always to point in the air and order someone to "close those windows!"

In those days, I had an absolute irrational fear of numbers. When I saw numbers on a paper, with mathematical symbols, it could turn my stomach, make my mouth dry and bring on a cold sweat all at once. So my work was full of frantic errors and crossings out. My work was never "a thing of beauty" in either presentation or content, and that set Eudoxus on my case ... relentlessly.

Recently the traditionally steep hilled school football field had been levelled. But the rock formation of the area meant that the playing field was littered with little shards of shale rock which would cut like razor if fell upon. There was no other way to remove this shale than to meticulously handpick it from the pitch piece by piece. One day, the entire school was out on the fields picking the shale. We did this on a regular basis until one day, miraculously, all the shale had been picked and our school had a new, level playing field.

On one of these days out picking shale, I finally lost it with Eudoxus. On this and previous days, he had kept hovering about directing (I believed) most of his instruction at me in particular and I tolerated this for quite a while, until one day in a field full of classmates, I exploded: "Why are you always picking on me?" I shouted and almost gave Eudoxus a heart attack.

Sadly, some years later, I later learnt, on return back to school after the summer holidays of the passing away of Mr Eudoxus. I came to see his persistence as a vain bid to try and impart to me some of the beauty in the world of numbers that he had appreciated, but that I would not learn to appreciate until my senior years. Today, I must admit, if it had not been for Eudoxus and my nurtured interest in mathematics, I would not have survived, as numbers have literally put bread on my table for the most of my working life.

The love of numbers led me to have the confidence to teach myself the rudiments of accounting, through direct work experience, attending short courses and eventually gaining an accounting qualification.

Let's be honest, many an accountant I have met wanted to be something else! A theatre director, a mathematician, a musician – I wanted to be full-time earth scientist, but after a research degree I ended up working in payroll and accountancy for the next twenty years, as my late father could have predicted.

My dad had wanted me, at first, to be an architect. When I went for the interview to study architecture at Avonshire Metropolitan University, I was asked to name an architect whose work I respected.

I had no clue. So I replied "John Poulson". The only architect I could name was the one in the news at the time being investigated for corruption and bribery.

So when that dream failed for my Dad (it wasn't *my* dream), he set sights on me becoming an accountant; whilst I dreamed of greater glories, perhaps making a breakthrough scientific discovery. But my dad had foreseen way back then that for me the prospect of becoming a middle aged accountant was more realistic than becoming a celebrated scientist, and even said as much.

With life's battering and disappointments, I had learnt to accept this fate...*my* fate. Not only that. I was going with the flow - of these forces that were shaping my working life. As I sat on the park bench,

listening to Zen's guide to practical financial accounting, as he sat beside me, I was hoping that he could deliver on his promise and help me complete a final piece of the jigsaw, by teaching me financial accounting and leading me to fulfil exactly what my dad had predicted.

We alternated with breaks from walking, sitting on park benches, admiring the greenery and the scenery as we went along. I decided not to interrupt the flow of Zen's practical exposition of financial accounting.

3

The Founding of the Pyramid Company

Nothing made Zen so animated and excited as have to explain and to be the centre of undivided attention: -

In this adventure of financial accounting we are set a problem:

FINANCIAL ACCOUNTS PROBLEM 1

You are required to produce the monthly financial accounts for April 2014 for the Pyramid Company Ltd (a small not- for- profit education company with just one worker) which is being started up from 1st April 2014 with a capital sum of £7,578, let's say. *Specifically, you are asked to arrive at the statement of profit and loss (income and expenditure) and the trial balance, and use these to draft the balance sheet.* For this first problem, please assume there are no debtors, prepayments, or accruals.

When we set up a business of course we will open our cash book as we describe more fully ahead. The first journal we write in our ledger is a double entry journal noting the capital amount of £7578. Capital is actually a liability and not an asset and is treated like a loan. In this case, it is treated as a loan from a director to the company. The double entry journal is as follows.

Opening Journal

Table 1 OPENING JOURNAL ENTRY

CODE	DETAILS	DR	CR
2300	CAPITAL – director loan *(credit the capital account)*		7578
1200	Bank – cash *(debit the bank account)*	7578	
	Total	7578	7578

The term "double entry" refers to the fact that every financial transaction has a giver and a receiver. So if the giver is assigned an account and the receiver is assigned an account, then one account must be credited and another debited in any transaction. We represent this as above, with the debit and credit columns balanced on the same amount £7578. Every journal that we write for the accounts must balance in this way. Most accounting software will not allow you to complete a journal unless the debit and credit columns balance.

To begin the financial accounts we provide the remainder of the information needed by the reader (for problem 1, and also problem 2 ahead). We provide:-

1) The income received and expenditure in April 2014 as below. (See Table A).
2) The Pyramid Company bank statement for the period 1st – 30th April 2014 (Table B).
3) The staff payroll summary for April 2014 (Table C).
4) The annual budget for Pyramid Company (Tables D and E).

Table A. PYRAMID COMPANY - April Income and Expenditure List for Data Entry into Computer Accounts Software

date	details	Expenditure £	Income £
1/4/14	AMNESTY - SO	8	
1/4/14	Orisa Press – accountancy fees	200	
3/4/14	BARNARDOS - SO	3	
4/4/14	Avonshire Youth FC fees Chq 1252	25	
4/4/14	BRITISH GAS -DD	21.11	
5/4/14	K. Da Silva chq	25	
8/4/14	CLOTHING -DD	25	
1/4/14	COUNCIL TAX - SO	82.89	
1/4/14	Directors loan		7578.06
7/4/14	DONATION - SO	30	
4/4/14	HP COMPUTER - DD	299	
16/4/14	INSURANCE - DD	34.49	
28/4/14	NET WAGES - APR	2450	
16/4/14	PHONE -DD	34.65	
29/4/14	PHONE - DD	43.51	
8/4/14	RENT - SO	454.83	
1/4/14	SAGE UK - DD	72.59	
3/4/14	SCOPE LTD - SO	9	

8/4/14	SUBSISTENCE - CASH	100	
10/4/14	SUBSISTENCE - CASH	50	
14/4/14	SUBSISTENCE - CASH	41.99	
16/4/14	SUBSISTENCE - CASH	81.99	
18/4/14	Book – PACE education	25	
22/4/14	SUBSISTENCE – CASH	100	
30/4/14	SUBSISTENCE – CASH	51.93	
28/4/14	SUBSISTENCE – CASH	80	
4/4/14	TRAVEL - DD	20	
14/4/14	TRAVEL - DD	20	
4/4/14	TRAVEL – BUS PASS - DD	20.2	
25/4/14	WATERAID - SO	11	

Table B. PYRAMID COMPANY - April Bank Statement

date	details	DR	CR	balance
01/04/2014	Directors loan		7578.06	7578.06
01/04/2014	AMNESTY - SO	8		7570.06
01/04/2014	COUNCIL TAX - SO	82.89		7487.17
				7487.17
01/04/2014	SAGE UK - DD	72.59		7414.58
03/04/2014	BARNARDOS - SO	3		7411.58

Date	Description	Amount		Balance
03/04/2014	SCOPE LTD - SO	9		7402.58
04/04/2014	Avonshire Youth FC fees Chq 1252	25		7377.58
04/04/2014	BRITISH GAS -DD	21.11		7356.47
				7356.47
04/04/2014	HP COMPUTER - DD	299		7057.47
04/04/2014	TRAVEL - DD	20		7037.47
04/04/2014	TRAVEL – BUS PASS -DD	20.2		7017.27
05/04/2014	K. D'Silva	25		6992.27
07/04/2014	DONATION - SO	30		6962.27
08/04/2014	CLOTHING -DD	25		6937.27
08/04/2014	RENT - SO	454.83		6482.44
08/04/2014	SUBSISTENCE - CASH	100		6382.44
10/04/2014	SUBSISTENCE - CASH	50		6332.44
14/04/2014	SUBSISTENCE - CASH	41.99		6290.45
14/04/2014	TRAVEL - DD	20		6270.45
16/04/2014	INSURANCE - DD	34.49		6235.96
16/04/2014	PHONE -DD	34.65		6201.31
16/04/2014	SUBSISTENCE - CASH	81.99		6119.32
22/04/2014	SUBSISTENCE – CASH	100		6019.32

25/04/2014	WATERAID - SO	11	6008.32
28/04/2014	NET WAGES - APR	2450	3558.32
28/04/2014	SUBSISTENCE – CASH	80	3478.32
29/04/2014	PHONE - DD	43.51	3434.81
30/04/2014	SUBSISTENCE – CASH	51.93	3382.88

Table C. PYRAMID COMPANY – APRIL PAYMENT SUMMARY PART 1

PYRAMID COMPANY - PAYMENT SUMMARY PART 1

Ref	NAME	TOTAL GROSS	TAXABLE GROSS	OTHER PAYMENTS	STUDENT LOAN	PAYE	EMPLOYEE NIC	EMPLOYER NIC	NET PAY
1	C. MAKELA	3241	3241	3241	0	481.2	309.6	256.04	2450.2
		3241	3241	3241	0	481.2	309.6	256.04	2450.2

Table D. Pyramid Company Annual Budget 2014-15

	2014-15 annual	
	Budget £	NOTES
INCOME		
National Academy of Sciences Grant	8,000	Grant commences 1st April 2014
The World Academy of Sciences	45,046	Grant commences 1st May 2014
Total Income	53046	
EXPENDITURE		
Gross Wages	43,164	
Rent and Rates	6,868	
Heat, Light and Power	253	
Motor Expenses	0	
Travelling and Entertainment	1,346	
Printing and Stationery	2,160	
Professional Fees	2,400	
Depreciation	96	
General Expenses	1,680	
Total Expenditure	57,968	

Table E. Pyramid Company Annual Budget 2014-15

PYRAMID
COMPANY
LTD   MONTH BY MONTH ANNUAL BUDGET
ANNUAL
BUDGET
2014-15

	APR	MAY	JUN	JUL	AUG	SEP	OCT	NOV	DEC	JAN	FEB	MAR	ANNUAL BUDGET £
INCOME													
National Academy of Sciences Grant	667	667	667	667	667	667	667	667	667	667	667	667	8000
The World Academy of Sciences	0	4095	4095	4095	4095	4095	4095	4095	4095	4095	4095	4095	45046
													53046
EXPENDITURE													
Gross Wages	3597	3597	3597	3597	3597	3597	3597	3597	3597	3597	3597	3597	43164
Rent and Rates	572	572	572	572	572	572	572	572	572	572	572	572	6868
Heat, Light and Power	21	21	21	21	21	21	21	21	21	21	21	21	253
Motor Expenses	0	0	0	0	0	0	0	0	0	0	0	0	0
Travel	112	112	112	112	112	112	112	112	112	112	112	112	1346
Printing and Stationery	180	180	180	180	180	180	180	180	180	180	180	180	2160
Profess-ional Fees	200	200	200	200	200	200	200	200	200	200	200	200	2400
Depreciat-ion	8	8	8	8	8	8	8	8	8	8	8	8	96
General Expenses	140	140	140	140	140	140	140	140	140	140	140	140	1680
													57968

4

The Chart of Accounts

We begin our work by printing out the chart of accounts (See table 2 below). The chart is a list of all the accounts and it is arranged conveniently so that the account types we use for the balance sheet (fixed assets, current assets, liabilities and profit and loss items) are in their respective separate code number ranges. For instance, we can broadly identify the code ranges of these account types

Table 2 Chart of Accounts Code Ranges

ACCOUNT CODE RANGE	ACOUNT TYPE
0010 to 0051	Fixed Assets
1001 to 1103	Current assets – debtors/stock
1200 to 1250	Currents assets – bank accounts
2100 to 2109	Liabilities – creditors and accruals
2200 to 2230	Liabilities - tax, NI, pensions
2300 to 2330	Liabilities – loans, mortgages etc
4000 to 4905	Profit & Loss – Income
5000 to 8205	Profit and loss - Expenditure

With this list, the trial balance, and profit and loss statement, we shall see, later on, that we can very easily draft the balance sheet. It is therefore the case that once we have arrived at the full trial balance; our work of producing the financial accounts is nearly complete.

In line with the IFRS (International Financial Reporting Standards), companies are required to report in a basic framework including 1)statement of financial position (i.e., balance sheet), 2) a statement of comprehensive income, 3) statement of changes in equity and a statement of cash flows. Our basic financial accounts report will therefore comprise of

- balance sheet (and notes),

- comprehensive statement of income, and

- statement of income and expenditure (and notes)

5

The Balance Sheet

In considering the problem of producing the April financial accounts for the Pyramid Company, we shall begin by giving the reader a preview of the resulting balance sheet the reader is expected to arrive at, effectively giving the reader the solution to the problem. This way, the reader can check they have understood the problem, as the balance sheet they draft must exactly be the one below in table 3, which for ease of reference is presented again in table 9, chapter 12, when we describe the drafting of this balance sheet for problem 1.

We note that the balance sheet is arranged in a format according to the basic account types described in the chart of accounts - table 2 - above (fixed and current assets, liabilities, profit and loss accounts). We take good note of these account types:

Fixed Assets –

In the first row, the balance sheet displays the "FIXED ASSETS" (here subdivided into leasehold improvements, office equipment and fittings and lastly computer equipment) brought forward at 1st April 2014, which is zero as the company is just starting. The second row shows the additions to equipment made in the year to date, which amounts to £299 for the purchase of a computer in April 2014.

The fourth row of the balance sheet we have the accumulated depreciation brought forward at 1st April 2014. The fifth row shows the depreciation charge in the year so far. As it is only April and the depreciation charge in April is just £8, this is the figure we find in the line for computer equipment. Later on we will cover the update of the fixed asset and depreciation schedule when we will include the

update for this new computer and its corresponding depreciation charge. The net book value is the cost of the computer less the amount of depreciation charge in the period; so net book value in row seven of the balance sheet is £291. Depreciation is essentially dealt with in the balance sheet as a reduction in the value of fixed assets.

Current Assets –

The only items falling under "CURRENT ASSETS" are the "cash at bank" and "cash in hand" items of £3158 and £454 respectively.

Table 3. BALANCE SHEET – PROBLEM 1

	PYRAMID COMPANY LTD			
	BALANCE SHEET AT 30 April 2014			
	£	£	£	£
	Leasehold Improvmnts	Office equip Fix & Fittings	Computer Equipment	TOTAL
FIXED ASSETS				
Cost brought forward 1.4.2014			0	0
Additions			299	299
			299	299
Depreciation brought forward 1.4.2014			0	0
Depreciation charge in the year			8	8
Accumulated Depreciation			8	8
Net book value			291	291
CURRENT ASSETS				
Debtors		Note 1	0	
Prepayments		Note 2	0	
Cash at Bank			3158	
Cash at Hand			454	
				3612
CREDITORS				
CAPITAL – directors loan				7578
Bank overdraft				
Trade creditors				
Accruals		Note 3		
PAYE/NIC and salaries				1147
Net wages control				
				8725
NET CURRENTS ASSETS				(5113)
NET ASSETS				(4822)
Represented by:				
	Balance b/f at 01/04/2014	Surplus/ (Deficit)	Prior Period Adjustments	Balance c/f at 30/04/14
Unrestricted Reserves				
RESTRICTED FUNDS	0	(4822)		(4822)
Net Surplus/Deficit	0	(4822)	0	(4822)

31

Creditors (Liabilities) –

The capital amount of £7578 is the amount used to start up the company and is treated as a director's loan. Also, we have unpaid tax and NI to HMRC (HM REVENUE & CUSTOMS) which constitutes a liability of £1147 (this is given by the sum of balances of PAYE control accounts shown in table 6 ahead).

Profit & Loss (Equity) –

The unmarked section at the bottom of the balance sheet below the line for net assets is the profit and loss section. What we term as "equity" is the net profit (or net loss). The profit and loss account has a zero balance brought forward at 1st April 2014. No income was received in April, but £4822 was spent. The profit and loss account therefore has a net deficit of £4822

The Assets-Liabilities-Equity (ALE) Equation –

So having appreciated the formatting of the balance sheet (table 3), we must remind ourselves of the formula that ensures our balance sheet actually balances. This formula will be presented in two ways to explain how/why we achieve a balance in the balance sheet and the trial balance. The first representation of this equation is

ASSETS – LIABILITIES = EQUITY   ....(1)

We shall remember this key formula by the acronym ALE. We note that the upper and lower sections of the balance sheet respectively are represented by the left hand (NET ASSETS) and right hand side (NET SURPLUS/DEFICIT) of the ALE equation. Taking the net values of each section of the balance sheet we see that indeed we have

ASSETS (fixed and current) – LIABILITIES (creditors) = EQUITY (net loss or deficit)

Substituting the numbers in the balance sheet (table 3) the reader may verify that

$$291 + 3612 - 8725 = -4822$$

The net assets of - £4822 are equal to the equity (net deficit) of - £4822.

In the second representation of the ALE equation, equation (1) is re-arranged and each side of the equation corresponds respectively to the debit (DR) and credit (CR) columns of the trial balance.

$$\text{ASSETS} = \text{LIABILITIES} + \text{EQUITY} \quad \dots\dots\dots\dots\dots\dots\dots\dots\dots\dots\dots\dots\dots(2)$$

So in the DR column of the trial balance we have fixed assets and current assets ; whilst in the CR column we have liabilities and equity. So the DR column of the trial balance will contain the value of all office equipment and furniture, etc, debtors, prepayments, bank account balances (unless these are negative, in which case these become a liability and fall in the CR column), petty cash, etc; whilst the CR column will contain our creditors and accruals, etc , and equity in line with the descriptions of assets and liabilities in table 3. The "EQUITY" in the above equation is the net surplus/deficit of the profits and losses (income and expenditure).

So the Assets-Liabilities-Equity equation shows us there is no mystery to why the trial balance balances - one of the wonders of accounting to a non-accountant! How all those seemingly "random" accounts lumped together manage to balance, looks initially surprising to one who studies a trial balance for the first time.

We shall see later on, in the final stages of preparing our financial accounts (chapter 12), how we draw up the balance sheet using our final trial balance (with the code ranges of the chart of accounts outlined in table 2) and profit and loss report.

6

The Donkey Work Begins

The Cash Book

We start work on the financial accounts proper, by undertaking the task of record keeping, which in the computer age entails data entry into some software or other. We recall that basic financial record keeping begins with the cash book. The cash book records all entries that go through the bank account. In the case of Pyramid Co. Ltd, we have only one bank account. But if we had more bank accounts, we would have to establish a separate cashbook for each account.

In the modern age there are so many computer software packages that enable you to input financial data. However, we do not lose sight of the fact that this is all based on the manual system, illustrated below. Our physical or digital cashbook should have plenty of columns to describe all the different sources of income and types of expenditure as below.

INCOME

DATE	REF	DETAILS	TOTAL	GRANTS	FEES	INTEREST	ETC

EXPENDITURE

DATE	PAYEE	CHQ NO	TOTAL	WAGES	RENT	PHONE	ETC

Data Inputting

The long process of preparing the financial accounts starts with the entry of all the data into the accounting system. In the days before computers all journals were written manually and the process would have required many more workers. Today, the powerful software can replace a team of workers so that a solitary accountant can perform the accounts for a small organisation. This however means we lose sight of some of the processes of accounting that are now hidden behind the software.

The reader is left to do the initial donkey work of entering the data in table A into their manual cashbook or accounting software. Once all of the data entries have been completed, we are ready to perform the April 2014 bank reconciliation for Pyramid.

7

The Bank Reconciliation

The bank reconciliation is performed regularly to make sure that the records of the organisation are accurate and also complete. The April bank reconciliation of the Pyramid Company was performed as below. Bank reconciliations nowadays are performed on various accounting software packages; but we consider the principles by completing our bank reconciliation for the Pyramid Co in April 2014 manually. The reconciliation is laid out as follows and it is assumed that the reader is familiar with the procedure of bank reconciliation.

PYRAMID COMPANY – BANK RECONCILIATION

Bank reconciliation as at 30th April 2014

	£
Balance brought fwd	0
Add receipts	7578
Less payments	4420
	_____
CASH BOOK BALANCE AT 30 APRIL 2014	3158

		£
Balance as per bank statement @ 30th April 2014		3383
Less: cheques not yet cleared		

Date	Cheque No.	
1/4/14	1264	200.00
18/4/14	1266	25.00

Add: receipts not yet cleared	_____
ADJUSTED BANK BALANCE	3158

The adjusted bank balance and the cash book balance at 30th April should be equal. We note this to be the case, and the bank reconciliation for Pyramid is duly completed as above.

The bank reconciliation above includes all financial transactions through the bank from 1st to 30th April 2014.

The reconciliation is started with the cashbook balance brought forward from the previous month. Since Pyramid Company is at its inception, the balance is zero. The only receipts are the director's loan to start up the company, which amounted to £7,578 paid into the bank. Subtracting the total payments or expenditure in the period from this gives us our cashbook balance of £3158.

We then note, lower down, that the bank reconciliation is completed when the April 30th bank statement balance of £3383, less the uncleared cheques 1264 and 1266, gives us an adjusted balance that agrees with the cashbook balance of £3158.

The uncleared cheques are highlighted as unreconciled transactions in the table ahead (Table 4).

TABLE 4 PYRAMID RECONCILED AND UNRECONCILED TRANSACTIONS

RECONCILED & UNRECONCILED BANK TRANSACTIONS	APRIL 2014	Unreconciled transactions (ref: chq 1264 and 1266) are shown shaded		AMOUNT £
DATE	REF			
18/04/2014	1265	Purchase Payment		82.89
01/04/2014	1264	Purchase Payment		200
18/04/2014	1266	Purchase Payment		25
01/04/2014	card 01	Purchase Payment		72.59
03/04/2014	DC3/4/1	Purchase Payment		100
03/04/2014	DC3/4/2	Purchase Payment		9
03/04/2014	DC/3/4/3	Purchase Payment		25
04/04/2014	DC4/4/1	Purchase Payment		299
04/04/2014	DC4/4/2	Purchase Payment		20
04/04/2014	DC/4/4/3	Purchase Payment		20.2
08/04/2014	DC/8/4/1	Purchase Payment		454.83
08/04/2014	DC8/4/2	Purchase Payment		8
08/04/2014	TRANS	Bank Transfer		50
14/04/2014	CARD01	Purchase Payment		20
14/04/2014	TRANS	Bank Transfer		41.99
16/04/2014	DD01	Purchase Payment		34.65
16/04/2014	TRANS	Bank Transfer		81.99
16/04/2014	DD01	Purchase Payment		34.65
22/04/2014	TRANS	Bank Transfer		100
25/04/2014	DC01	Purchase Payment		30
25/04/2014	DD02	Purchase Payment		11
28/04/2014	CARD01	Purchase Payment		25
28/04/2014	SO01	Purchase Payment		25
28/04/2014	NET WAGE	NET WAGES - CAM APRIL		2450
28/04/2014	TRANS	Bank Transfer		80
30/04/2014	CARD01	Purchase Payment		51.93
30/04/2014	SO01	Purchase Payment		3
29/04/2014	DD01	Purchase Payment		43.51
30/04/2014	DD01	Purchase Payment		21.11
01/04/2014	JNL00002	DIRECTORS LOAN - CAPITAL INPUT	7578.06	

8

Wages and Salaries Journal

We recall from the problem statement, that the Pyramid have one employee, named Ms Constance Makela, whose payslip summary for April 2014 is as follows

Table 5. WAGES AND SALARIES

Name	Total Gross	PAYE	Employee NIC	Employer NIC	NET PAY
C. Makela	3241	481.20	309.60	356.04	2450.20

We use this summary to prepare the salaries journal and enter this into our manual books or accounting software:-

Table 6. Salaries Journal

Code	Details	DR	CR
7000	Salaries (Gross pay)	3241	
7006	Salaries (EER NI)	356.04	
2210	PAYE control acct (tax)		481.20
2211	PAYE control acct (Employee NIC)		309.60
2212	PAYE control account (Employer NIC)		356.04
2220	Net Pay		2450.20
		3597.04	3597.04

In the Salaries Journal above, table 6, we note that the balances in the PAYE control accounts represent unpaid tax, and national insurance (NI) due to the HMRC (HM Revenue and Customs) for the month of April 2014. The HMRC liability for April is therefore the sum of the PAYE control account balances for tax, employee NI and employer NI, which amounts to £1147 (to the nearest pound).

9

Debtors, Prepayments and Accruals (Problem 1)

Normally we would be expected to update the debtors, prepayment and accruals schedules. In problem 1, we assume there are no debtors, prepayments or accruals to make things very simple. So we must return to the topic of debtors, prepayments and accruals when we consider the solution to problem 2 ahead. [See ahead, Debtors, Prepayments and Accruals (Problem 2), CHAPTER 13].

10

Depreciation

The last of the journals to be drafted is that for depreciation. We first calculate the depreciation charge for the month and then accordingly update the depreciation schedule (table 7). We note that the only fixed asset purchase made in the year to date is a computer bought for the sum of £299. We choose to use the method of Straight Line over a period of 3 years (this happens to be the period of the National Academy of Science funding) so that the equipment depreciates at the rate of 299/36 = £8.31 per month precisely.

In table 7 we see that as the company is new, there are no brought forward fixed assets (column 3) or depreciation (column 9) at 31st March 2014. We enter the sum of £299 in the additions (column 4) of the depreciation schedule. We proceed to calculate the depreciation as above and complete the schedule entry. With this information on a monthly basis we can expect to be keeping the fixed assets register up to date.

Table 7.

PYRAMID COMPANY - DEPRECIATION SCHEDULE AT 30 APRIL 2014

	1	2	3	4	5	6	At Apr 2014 DEPRECIATION CALCS		9	10	11	12	13	14	15
Date of purchase	Detail	Depreciation rate	Cost b/f	Additions	disposals	cost c/f	depreciation per month	number of months expired	depreciation b/f	disposals	depreciation	total dep'n	net book value B/f	net book value c/f	depreciation c/f
			Mar-14			Apr-14			Mar-14		Apr-14	30/04/20114	Mar-14	Apr-14	Apr-14
COMPUTER COSTS:-															
04/04/2014	Office Equipment - HP computer	3 year straight line	0.00	£299.00	0	£299.00	8.31		0.00	0	8.31	8.31	0	291	8.31
			0.00	299.00	0.00	299.00	8.31	0.00	0.00	0.00	8.31	8.31	0.00	0.00	8.31
			0.00												

So, using the numbers from our completed depreciation schedule, we can now draft the final journal for depreciation,

Table 8. Depreciation Journal

Code Details	DR	CR
8004 Depreciation charges	8.31	
0031 Depreciation B/F		8.31
	8.31	8.31

We then enter our journal into our manual or computerised accounts system.

11

The Trial Balance (Problem 1)

Once all of the work above has been done, it remains for us to make one final check to ensure no omissions have been made and to print out our final trial balance. This is the trial balance we will use to draft the accounts for problem 1, so it must be correct. The final trial balance for problem 1 is given below.

FINANCIAL ACCOUNTS PROBLEM 1
- THE TRIAL BLANACE AT 30 APRIL FOR PYRAMID COMPANY

CODE		DR	CR
0030	Office Equipment	299	
0031	Office Equipment Depreciation B/F		8
1200	Bank Current Account	3157.72	
1230	Petty Cash	453.98	
2210	P.A.Y.E.		481
2211	National Insurance		666.04
2300	Loans		7578.06
7000	Gross Wages	3597.04	
7100	Rent	454.83	
7103	General Rates	82.89	
7104	Premises Insurance	34.65	
7201	Gas	21.11	
7400	Travelling	60.2	
7406	Subsistence	51.93	
7502	Telephone	78.16	
7504	Office Stationery	72.59	
7505	Books etc.	25	
7603	Professional Fees	200	
8004	Office Equipment Depreciation	8	
8200	Donations	86	
8201	Subscriptions	25	
8202	Clothing Costs	25	
9998	Suspense Account		
9999	Mispostings Account		
		8733.1	8733.1

PYRAMID COMPANY LTD
APRIL 2014 - INCOME AND EXPENDITURE STATEMENT
(PROBLEM 1)

INCOME
National Academy of Sciences Grant   0

                                                                0

EXPENDITURE
                                                          3597.04
Gross Wages
Rent and Rates   572.37
Heat, Light and Power   21.11
Motor Expenses   0
Travelling and Entertainment   112.13
Printing and Stationery   175.75
Professional Fees   200
Depreciation   8
General Expenses   136
                                                           4822.4

NET SURPLUS/DEFICIT   -4822.4

From this trial balance, and the Chart of Accounts in table 4, we are able to draft the balance sheet in table 5 as follows:-

On the balance sheet please note that the sequence of occurrence of the items is almost the same as on the trial balance (the reader should tick and tally the items on the trial balance with the corresponding areas of the balance sheet):

- At the top of the balance sheet we have the fixed assets – the computer purchase cost of £299 less the depreciation of £8 (precisely £8.31) gives us the net book value of £291.

- This is followed by the current assets – no debtors; no prepayments; £3158 cash at bank; £454 petty cash in hand.

- This then followed by the creditors - the capital of £7578 to start up the company, recorded as a directors loan; the HMRC liability of £1147 (the total of PAYE control accounts in the salaries journal, table 6) .

- At the base of the balance sheet is the statement of equity, a deficit of - £4822, which is the net result on the trial balance of summing all items from code 7000 down to the 9999 for the suspense account. We note that -£4822 is the net figure stated in our profit and loss (income and expenditure) statement above.

Table 9. BALANCE SHEET – PROBLEM 1

PYRAMID COMPANY LTD
BALANCE SHEET AT 30 April 2014

	£ Leasehold Improvmnts	£ Office equip Fix & Fittings	£ Computer Equipment	£ TOTAL
FIXED ASSETS				
Cost brought forward 1.4.2014			0	0
Additions			299	299
			299	299
Depreciation brought forward 1.4.2014			0	0
Depreciation charge in the year			8	8
Accumulated Depreciation			8	8
Net book value			291	291
CURRENT ASSETS				
Debtors		Note 1	0	
Prepayments		Note 2	0	
Cash at Bank			3158	
Cash at Hand			454	
				3612
CREDITORS				
CAPITAL – directors loan				7578
Bank overdraft				
Trade creditors				
Handling Account				
Accruals		Note 3		
PAYE/NIC and salaries				1147
Net wages control				
				8725
NET CURRENTS ASSETS				(5113)
NET ASSETS				(4822)

Represented by:

	Balance b/f at 01/04/2014	Surplus/ (Deficit)	Prior Period Adjustments	Balance c/f at 30/04/14
Unrestricted Reserves				
RESTRICTED FUNDS	0	(4822)		(4822)
Net Surplus/Deficit	0	(4822)	0	(4822)

12

Debtors, Prepayments and Accruals (Problem 2)

As promised, we return to complete our study of debtors, prepayments and accruals by simple example.

In Financial accounts Problem 2, we are asked to perform precisely the same financial accounts for April in problem 1, with the added challenge that we allow the inclusion of a debtor, a prepayment and an accrual as detailed ahead shortly:-

FINANCIAL ACCOUNTS PROBLEM 2

You are required to produce the monthly financial accounts for April 2014 for the pyramid company ltd (a small not- for- profit education company with just one worker) which is being started up from 1ˢᵗ April 2014 with a capital sum of £7,578, let's say. You are asked to arrive at the statement of profit and loss (income and expenditure) and the trial balance, and use these to draft the balance sheet as in problem 1. But in problem 2, in addition to this, please assume one debtor, one prepayment and one accrual as detailed below, and complete the balance sheet notes. [An additional exercise introduced by Zen to introduce the production of basic management accounts was to produce an income expenditure report with explanation notes of variances from the budget for the period].

We proceed to complete the financial accounts for problem 2 as we have done for problem 1, with the only differences being the additional request to compare the actual income and expenditure against budget as an introduction to preparing the most basic management accounts (we leave this till last – SEE CHAPTER 14); and the inclusion of one debtor, one prepayment and one accrual as follows.

Debtor – National Academy of Sciences Grant

The Pyramid has received a grant from the National Academy of Sciences of £8,000 for the year 2014-15 starting 1st April 2014. The grant had not been received as at 30th April 2014, giving us a debtor for one month of the grant amounting to 8000/12 = £667

We write a corresponding debtor journal for our manual system or enter this into our accounting software as follows:

Debtor Journal

Code	Details	DR	CR
4000	NAS account		667
1100	Debtors account	667	
		667	667

Prepayment – Tetlow County Council Annual Company Parking Permit

The only prepayment is due to an exorbitant £2400 annual parking permit for the Company paid for on 1st April 2014 to the local council. This amounts to a prepayment of 11 months or 11x(2400/12) = £2200

As we did for debtors, we write a corresponding journal for our manual system or enter this into our accounting software as follows:

Prepayment journal

Code	Details	DR	CR
7400	Travel (P&L acct)		2200
1103	Prepayments acct	2200	
		2200	2200

Accrual – Westbridge Accountants Annual Payroll Service Charge

The only amount accruing in the month is that due to a £1200 annual payroll service charge to West bridge Accountants for which a half year invoice is issued in November. However, one month of this annual charge has been accrued or equivalently 1200/12 = £100 at 30th April 2014.

We write a corresponding journal for the £100 accrual for our manual system or enter this into our accounting software as follows:

Accruals journal

Code	Details	DR	CR
7601	Payroll & Acctcy (P&L acct)	100	
2109	Accruals account		100
		100	100

Including these changes (one debtor, one prepayment and one accrual) will not change our bank reconciliation, but will change the profit and loss report and trial balance from which we must now draft the final balance sheet and complete the financial accounts for problem 2. Including these changes alters our profit and loss (income and expenditure) report to the following:-

PYRAMID COMPANY LTD

APRIL 2014 - INCOME AND EXPENDITURE STATEMENT
(PROBLEM 2)

INCOME

National Academy of Sciences Grant	667
	667

EXPENDITURE

Gross Wages	3597.04
Rent and Rates	572.37
Heat, Light and Power	21.11
Travelling and Entertainment	-2087.87
Printing and Stationery	175.75
Professional Fees	300
Depreciation	8
General Expenses	136
	2722.4

NET SURPLUS/DEFICIT	-2055.40

And the trial balance is also accordingly revised to

FINANCIAL ACCOUNTS PROBLEM 2
- THE TRIAL BLANACE AT 30 APRIL FOR PYRAMID COMPANY

		DR	CR
0030	Office Equipment	299	
0031	Office Equipment Depreciation B/F		8
1100	Debtors Control Account	667	
1103	Prepayments	2200	
1200	Bank Current Account	3157.72	
1230	Petty Cash	453.98	
2109	Accruals		100
2210	P.A.Y.E.		481
2211	National Insurance		666.04
2300	Loans		7578.06
4001	National Academy of Sciences - Grant		667
7000	Gross Wages	3597.04	
7100	Rent	454.83	
7103	General Rates	82.89	
7104	Premises Insurance	34.65	
7201	Gas	21.11	
7400	Travelling		2139.8
7406	Subsistence	51.93	
7502	Telephone	78.16	
7504	Office Stationery	72.59	
7505	Books etc.	25	
7601	Audit and Accountancy Fees	100	
7603	Professional Fees	200	
8004	Office Equipment Depreciation	8	
8200	Donations	86	
8201	Subscriptions	25	
8202	Clothing Costs	25	
8203	Training Costs		
9998	Suspense Account		
9999	Mispostings Account		
		11639.9	11639.9

13

The Final Trial Balance and Balance Sheet (Problem 2)

"From this revised trial balance and P&L (profit and loss) statement we are able to draft the following balance sheet in table 10".

I could sense at this point that having ploughed through the hard work rigorously Zen was beginning to feel the excitement of approaching the finish line along this arduous journey into financial accounting. I had remained silent throughout, as if barely present; but miraculously, Zen had enabled me to understand EVERYTHING. I myself was captured by the excitement of approaching the close. It meant a lot to me; perhaps, it would change my job prospects, if not my life.

"On the balance sheet (table 10) please note that the sequence of occurrence of the items is almost the same as on the trial balance above in chapter 12:

- At the top of the balance sheet we have the fixed assets – the computer purchased for £299 less the depreciation of £8 (precisely £8.31).

- This is followed by the current assets – debtors of £667 (NAS); prepayments to Tetlow Council of £2,200; £3158 cash at bank; £454 petty cash in hand.

  This is then followed by the creditors - an accrual of £100 to the payroll agents, Westbridge Accountants; the capital of £7578 to start up the company, recorded as a directors loan; the HMRC liability of £1147 given by the sum of PAYE control account balances shown in table 6, the wages and salaries Journal, back in chapter 8. These accounts hold the amount respectively of tax, employer's national insurance contribution (NIC) and employee's NIC owed to HMRC, as Pyramid Company has yet to pay (and enter the payments for these amounts in its accounting system).

- At the base of the balance sheet is the statement of equity, a deficit of - £2055, which is the net result on the trial balance of summing all items from code 4001 down to the 9999 for the suspense account. We note that £2055 is the net figure (deficit) stated in our profit and loss (income and expenditure) statement in the previous chapter (12)".

Zen had now explained clearly to me all the features of the balance sheet for the financial accounts problem 2. It now remained to complete the final tasks before one could present the April 2014 financial accounts. Actually, I was confident enough to complete the work myself for problem 2, working patiently through the drafting of the balance sheet again, unaided, with my pencil, scrap paper and calculator. The remaining tasks I noted in accordance with problem 2 (chapter 12) were:-

- Completion of balance sheet notes

- Completion of comprehensive income statement

- Completion of income and expenditure statement (with explanatory notes on significant variations between actual and budgeted expenditure).

I went on to complete the balance sheet and notes (as presented in the final two pages ahead), and in so doing completed my first set of financial accounts. It was, in my eyes, a significant achievement: a thing of beauty and a joy forever.

Table 10. BALANCE SHEET – PROBLEM 2

PYRAMID COMPANY LTD
BALANCE SHEET AT 30 April 2014

	£ Leasehold Improvmnts	£ Office equip Fix & Fittings	£ Computer Equipment	£ TOTAL
FIXED ASSETS				
Cost brought forward 1.4.2014			0	0
Additions			299	299
			299	299
Depreciation brought forward 1.4.2014			0	0
Depreciation charge in the year			8	8
Accumulated Depreciation			8	8
Net book value			291	291
CURRENT ASSETS				
Debtors		Note 1	667	
Prepayments		Note 2	2200	
Cash at Bank			3158	
Cash at Hand			454	
				6479
CREDITORS				
CAPITAL – directors loan				7578
Bank overdraft				
Trade creditors				
Handling Account				
Accruals		Note 3		100
PAYE/NIC and salaries				1147
Net wages control				
				8825
NET CURRENTS ASSETS				(2346)
NET ASSETS				(2055)

Represented by:

	Balance b/f at 01/04/2014	Surplus/ (Deficit)	Prior Period Adjustments	Balance c/f at 30/04/14
Unrestricted Reserves **RESTRICTED FUNDS (NAS, etc)**	0	(2055)		(2055)
Net Surplus/Deficit	0	(2055)	0	(2055)

PYRAMID COMPANY LTD
Month ended 30th April 2014
BALANCE SHEET NOTES

NOTE 1   **DEBTORS**

Apr-14	National Academy of Sciences	667
		667

NOTE 2   **PREPAYMENTS**

Parking permit -	Tetlow Council	
Invoice £2400 from 1/4/14 - 31/3/15	prepay 11/12 months	2200
(£2400 annual parking permit for the Company paid for on 1st April 2014 to the local council. This amounts to a prepayment of 11 months or 11x(2400/12) = £2200 At 30/4/14)		
		2200

NOTE 3   **ACCRUALS**

		Bal b/f	Adjustment	Bal c/f
Payroll - (1/12 months of	Westbridge Accountants plc Annual fee of £1200)	0	100	100
		0	100	100

14

Epilogue: Simple Management Accounts

In bringing our training session to an end, Zen acknowledged that in the final additional task given in Problem 2, the requested comparison of actual performance against budget represented the beginnings of a journey into management accounting. The complete exposition would be left for another day, he promised. But for now, it was enough to note that some basic management accounts reports (such as those used in small enterprises), merely entailed the comparison of actual income and expenditure against a pre-planned annual budget, and an analysis of the variances and the reasons for them, in order to aid management decision-making.

PYRAMID COMPANY LTD APRIL 2014 - INCOME AND EXPENDITURE STATEMENT (PROBLEM 2)		APRIL		2014-15 annual Budget	
	ACTUAL	BUDGET	VARIANCE	£	NOTES
INCOME					
National Academy of Sciences Grant	667	667	0	8,000	Grant commences 1st April 2014
The World Academy of Sciences	0	0	0	45,046	Grant commences 1st May 2014
	667	667	667	53,046	
EXPENDITURE					
Gross Wages	3,597	3,597	0	43,164	
Rent and Rates	572	572	0	6,868	
Heat, Light and Power	21	21	0	253	
Travelling	-2,088	112	2,200	1,346	
Printing and Stationery	176	180	4	2,157	
Professional Fees	300	200	-100	2,400	
Depreciation	8	8	0	96	
General Expenses	136	140	4	1,680	
	2,722	4,831	2,108	57,965	

NET SURPLUS/DEFICIT	2055.4

The level of variance regarded as significant will be a matter for the particular organisation. In the not-for- profit sector, a difference of more than 10 or 15 percent of the budgeted amount may merit an accompanying note to explain the reason(s) for the variance, which is arrived at by subtracting the actual income or expenditure from the corresponding budget income or expenditure.

The notes on variances between the budget and the actual income and expenditure exceeding 15% are as above. From the pre-planned budget for Pyramid Company Ltd, shown in a month by month format in table E, we see there is a shortfall in April due to lack of income to cover costs; whereas in May the World Academy of Sciences grant commences and will help cover organisational costs. The annual budget predicts a shortfall of £4922. It is hoped that by implementing cost cutting on items such as stationery, travel and general expenses, the board of Pyramid will reduce this figure over the course of the year. However, the scope for cost cutting is limited and the need for some fundraising is implied if Pyramid is not to end the year with a small deficit.

We may add columns to the income and expenditure statement to also report on the comparison between actual and budget figures for the year to date, as well as for the current period (month or quarter) being reported. An example of such a report is presented below, showing the comparison between May 2014 actual and budgeted figures, as well as the comparison between the year-to-date (YTD) actual and YTD budgeted figures for expenditure and income. The year-to-date figures are cumulative figures summing all the corresponding figures of the months to date (i.e., April plus May, in the instance below). We note from the month by month budget (table E) that by May 2014 we are due to have received the first instalment of The World Academy of Sciences Funding of £4095 to ameliorate our cash flow situation.

PYRAMID COMPANY LTD

MAY 2014 - INCOME AND EXPENDITURE STATEMENT

	MAY ACTUAL	MAY BUDGET	VARIANCE	YTD ACTUAL	YTD BUDGET	YTD VARIANCE	2014-15 annual Budget £
INCOME							
National Academy of Sciences Grant	667	667	0	1,334	1,334	0	8,000
The World Academy of Sciences	4,095	4,095	0	4,095	4,095	0	45,046
	4,762	4,762	0	5,429	5,429	0	53,046
EXPENDITURE							
Gross Wages	3,597	3,597	0	7194	7,194	0	43,164
Rent and Rates	546	572	26	1,118	1,145	27	6,868
Heat, Light and Power	21	21	0	42	42	0	253
Travelling	200	112	-88	-1,888	224	2,112	1,346
Printing and Stationery	13	180	167	189	360	171	2,160
Professional Fees	0	200	200	300	400	100	2,400
Depreciation	8	8	0	16	16	0	96
General Expenses	55	140	85	191	280	89	1,680
	4,440	4,831	390	7162	9,661	2,499	57,968